Ulysses S. Grant

Ulysses S. Grant

Janet Riehecky

AMERICA'S
18TH
PRESIDENT

Children's Press®
A Division of Scholastic Inc.
New York / Toronto / London / Auckland / Sydney
Mexico City / New Delhi / Hong Kong
Danbury, Connecticut

Library of Congress Cataloging-in-Publication Data

Riehecky, Janet, 1953–
    Ulysses S. Grant / by Janet Riehecky.
      p. cm.—(Encyclopedia of presidents. Second series)
    Summary: A biography of the eighteenth president of the United States,
with information on his childhood, family, political career, presidency,
and legacy.
Includes bibliographical references and index.
  ISBN 0-516-22868-4
   1. Grant, Ulysses S. (Ulysses Simpson), 1822–1885—Juvenile literature.
2. Presidents—United States—Biography—Juvenile literature. [1. Grant,
Ulysses S. (Ulysses Simpson), 1822–1885. 2. Presidents.] I. Title. II. Series.
E672.R54 2004
973.8'2'092—dc22   2003015940

Contents

Chapter 1

Quiet Beginning

When Ulysses Grant was a boy, he was a small, skinny child, serious and sensitive. He was not good at sports and was only an average student. The one talent he did have was for training and riding horses. No one suspected that this quiet boy would become his country's most famous general or that he would be elected president of the United States. Yet in his lifetime he became one of the country's most admired heroes, one who would lead vast armies to victory and do his best to bring a divided country back together.

He was born Hiram Ulysses Grant on April 27, 1822, in Point Pleasant, Ohio, along the banks of the Ohio River near Cincinnati. His parents were Jesse and Hannah Simpson Grant. Shortly after his birth, the family moved to Georgetown, Ohio, about 15 miles (24 kilometers) to the east. Grant was the oldest child in his family, but by the

Grant was born in this small house in Point Pleasant, Ohio, near the Ohio River. He was named Hiram Ulysses.

time he was ten, he had a younger brother and two younger sisters. Another brother and a sister were born when he was a teenager.

Grant's father, Jesse Grant, was a farmer and a *tanner*, a tradesman who treated animal hides, turning them into leather. His father may have hoped that young Hiram Ulysses would someday take over the tannery, but Grant never showed much interest in the messy, smelly processing of animal hides. He did not like slaughtering animals and refused even to go hunting. The sight of blood made him sick.

The one thing Grant did love was horses. When he was just a toddler, he played in the stables and even swung on the horses' tails without any fear of being hurt by them. By the time he was five, he could ride a horse, and at eight he could handle a wagon and team. By age eleven he did all the work on the farm that involved horses. He had a mysterious connection with them and could control and train them without ever raising his voice. As his skill became known, local farmers brought their colts to him to be trained.

Jesse Grant had very little education, and he was determined that his sons would have a better chance to learn. Hiram Ulysses began his education in a one-room schoolhouse in Georgetown. Later his father sent him to nearby boarding schools. The teachers in these schools often knew little more than the students.

A Bargain?

Young Grant was less successful dealing with people than with horses. When he was about eight years old, he convinced his father to let him buy a colt from one of their neighbors. The man wanted $25. Grant's father gave him detailed instructions to get the horse for less. The boy trustingly told the neighbor everything his father had told him—to offer $20; if that wasn't accepted, to offer $22.50; and if that wasn't acceptable to offer $25. The neighbor must have smiled at the boy's innocence. He sold Grant the horse for $25.

☆ ☆ ☆

However, Grant was not very interested in his studies and didn't care that he didn't learn much. He was a small, shy boy who made few friends.

In his *Memoirs*, Grant described his childhood as "uneventful." His parents expected him to work hard, but they also allowed him the freedom to go fishing, swimming, or ice-skating in the winter. Sometimes he took a horse and rode off to visit his grandparents, who lived about 15 miles (24 km) away.

West Point

In the fall of 1838, 16-year-old Hiram Ulysses was attending a boarding school in Ripley, Ohio. While he was at home for the Christmas holidays, his father received an official letter and announced proudly that his oldest son had received

Grant spent his boyhood in this home in Georgetown, Ohio, about 15 miles (24 km) east of his birthplace.

an appointment to attend the United States Military Academy at West Point, New York. Young Grant was surprised, since he had not known his father had applied for the appointment. He knew that the Military Academy had high standards and was not confident that he could succeed there. He was not a good student, and although he was strong, he was small, still only 5 feet 1 inch (1.55 meters) and

What's in a Name?

When Grant was born, he was named Hiram Ulysses. As a boy, he was usually called Ulysses or "Lyss." Because he was always called by his middle name, he resolved to enter his name at West Point as Ulysses Hiram Grant. However, when he arrived there, he found school officials had already changed his name. The congressman who had arranged his appointment knew that Grant's mother's maiden name was Simpson and assumed that Simpson was his middle name. The West Point position could be filled only by someone named Ulysses S. Grant. Grant tried twice to get his name changed, but he never succeeded. Finally, he just accepted the name, using the new middle initial for the rest of his life. His classmates at West Point used his initials to make a nickname for him. They called him Uncle Sam Grant, or just Sam.

☆ ☆ ☆

weighed only 117 pounds (53 kilograms). Grant's father didn't argue with him. He just said he thought Grant should go, and Grant went.

In the spring of 1839, Grant headed for West Point. In his *Memoirs* he remembers wishing there might be a railroad or steamship accident. He wanted to be slightly injured—not badly, just enough to make him unable to attend. Since there was no accident, he wrote, "I had to face the music."

That first summer was very difficult. To help students learn to cope with conditions they might experience in a war, they were given few comforts and bad food. Grant wrote to a cousin that he slept two months on a single pair of blankets. In addition, he found it hard to conform to the rigid discipline. He received many *demerits*, or bad marks on his permanent record, for such things as bad posture, buttons unbuttoned, marching out of step, and being late to class.

Grant did love the countryside around West Point. The U.S. Military Academy is perched on high cliffs overlooking the Hudson River. Its lands included steep, rugged hills with trails that challenged even experienced horsemen.

During his earlier school days, Grant had always done well in simple mathematics. At the academy, he discovered higher math and continued to do very well. In other courses, however, he was only an average student and preferred reading novels to studying. Unlike many of his classmates, he was not interested in an army career. If he could graduate, he hoped he could gain appointment as a junior math teacher at the academy for a few years, then find a teaching position in a college.

In his third term at West Point, Grant was promoted to sergeant, but he received so many demerits that he spent his fourth term there as a private. In June 1843, Grant graduated 21st out of 39 students. It was not a very good ranking, but more than half of the students he started with didn't graduate at all. He continued to excel at horsemanship. At the graduation exercises, he set a high jump record that stood for 25 years.

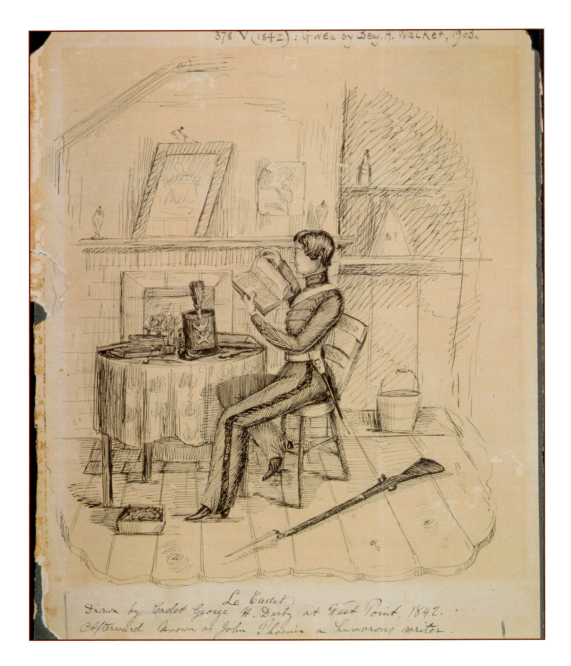

A sketch of a cadet's room at the U.S. Military Academy at West Point about the time Grant was a student there.

Grant hoped to get an assignment with the *cavalry*, the military units that fought on horseback, but there were no positions open. Instead he was assigned to the *infantry*, a unit of foot soldiers. His first assignment as a U.S. Army officer was to the Jefferson Barracks, a military post 10 miles (16 km) south of St. Louis, Missouri.

Before reporting to their posts, all the cadets received a three-month leave of absence. Grant returned to Ohio. While he was there, his new uniform was delivered. He put it on and rode on horseback into Cincinnati, expecting that he would receive much admiration. Instead, a young boy, barefoot and dirty, laughed at him. Even worse, when he returned home, he found a stable attendant dressed up in an imitation uniform parading about, getting big laughs. Grant felt humiliated. From then on he had a great dislike for fancy military uniforms.

Julia

One of Grant's roommates at West Point was Frederick Dent, whose family lived just outside St. Louis. Fred Dent urged Grant to visit them. The Dent plantation, called White Haven, was large and prosperous. Dent's father was known as "Colonel" Dent, though he had never served in the military. He owned 18 slaves and was a fierce defender of slavery.

Grant's family had always been against slavery, but Grant found he enjoyed discussing politics with Colonel Dent. In February 1844, he met the Dents' oldest daughter, 18-year-old Julia, who had returned home from boarding school. Julia was not particularly pretty, but Grant found her lively and charming. She loved riding as much as Grant did, and the two were soon taking long rides together.

About the first of May, Grant received a 20-day leave to visit his parents. While he was away, his regiment was ordered to Louisiana. Grant returned to the Jefferson Barracks and was ordered to board a steamboat and catch up with his regiment. He knew he had to see Julia before leaving, and made a special request for a few days' extra time. His commanding officer granted him a week's leave.

He set out for the Dent plantation on horseback. On the way, he was stopped by a small creek swollen with rainwater. In his *Memoirs*, Grant wrote, "One of my superstitions had always been when I started to go anywhere, or to do anything, not to turn back, or stop until the thing intended was accomplished." He plunged into the water and was caught by the current. It swept both horse and rider downstream. He could easily have drowned, but he was finally able to urge the horse up the other bank. He was safely across—and thoroughly wet.

Grant met Julia Dent in 1844, and they were married in 1848.

When he arrived at the Dent plantation, Grant borrowed some dry clothes from Julia's brother, then went to meet her. During the week, he escorted Julia to a wedding at which she was a bridesmaid. On the way, he told her that he loved her and that life would be "insupportable" without her. He asked her to marry him. She was only 18 and wasn't sure about marriage. She told him that she thought it would be charming to be engaged, but not to be married. He had to settle for this. He gave her his class ring, and she gave him a lock of her hair.

Then Ulysses Grant went off to join his regiment.

Off to War

In 1844, the independent republic of Texas had requested to be *annexed* by the United States, or made a part of that country. Long a territory of Mexico, Texas had revolted in 1836 and had become independent. Now it was hoping to become a state in the United States. In the presidential election that fall, Democrat James K. Polk was elected partly because he favored annexing Texas. Congress acted even before he took office in March 1845, and by the end of the year, the republic was admitted as a new state.

Mexico had never agreed to give up Texas, and it believed that the state was claiming Mexican lands it had no right to. It threatened to go to war to protect the disputed territory. President Polk announced he would protect Texas territory even if it meant war. Grant's regiment stayed in Louisiana into 1845, ready in case war broke out. Grant didn't mind this long, quiet period. Since entering West Point, he had grown to 5 feet 7 inches (1.70 m), and gained weight. In his last term, however, he suffered from an illness that brought his weight back down to 117 pounds (53 kg). Now, long days in the Louisiana sunshine helped him recover his health.

In September of 1845, his regiment became part of a large Army of Occupation at Corpus Christi, Texas, at the edge of the territory claimed by both Mexico and the United States. The commanding officer was Brigadier General Zachary Taylor, an experienced and respected army commander. Grant studied Taylor's style of leadership. Taylor maintained strict discipline, but made a point of getting to know all of his officers and many of the enlisted men. He often walked through the camp, making casual conversation. He didn't make speeches, but instead communicated his orders in a few well-chosen words. He dressed for comfort, not for display. As Grant would learn in the course of the U.S.-Mexican War, Taylor also faced dangers in battle calmly and confidently. When Grant became a military commander in the Civil War, he modeled his style and behavior after that of Zachary Taylor.

The huge encampment of the U.S. Army at Corpus Christi, Texas, in 1845, at the edge of disputed territory with Mexico.

Though Grant had nothing but praise for the army in which he served, he did not approve of the war itself. He believed that President Polk was eager to provoke a war with Mexico in order to gain huge new territories from it. In his *Memoirs*, he wrote, "For myself, I was bitterly opposed to [the annexation of Texas], and to this day regard the war as one of the most unjust ever waged by a stronger against a weaker nation." However, he was a soldier and followed orders, keeping his personal opinions to himself.

In early 1846, the army at Corpus Christi was ordered into the territory claimed by Texas and Mexico and began building a fort on the river known as the Rio Grande. Mexican troops crossed the Rio Grande and ambushed a U.S. scouting party. Soon afterward, on May 13, 1846, the United States officially declared war on Mexico.

In September 1846, General Taylor pushed across the Rio Grande and attacked the Mexican city of Monterrey. After several days of fighting, the army pushed its way into the city. Grant's regiment was in the thick of the fighting, and ammunition was running low. Someone had to take a message through the streets back to headquarters requesting the needed supplies, and Grant's commander asked for a volunteer. Grant immediately offered. He looped one arm

Fast Facts

THE U.S.-MEXICAN WAR

Who: The United States and Mexico

When: The U.S. Congress declared war against Mexico on May 13, 1846. Fighting ended in September 1847. The Treaty of Guadalupe Hidalgo was signed on February 2, 1848.

Why: When the U.S. made Texas, a former territory of Mexico, a state in 1845, Mexico threatened war. U.S. troops entered territory claimed by both nations and were attacked by Mexican forces in April 1846.

Where: The U.S. drove Mexican forces out of Texas and captured Monterrey in northern Mexico. They also captured parts of present-day New Mexico and California. In early 1847, a U.S. force landed at Veracruz, on Mexico's Gulf Coast, and fought its way to Mexico City. The Mexican capital was occupied in September, ending the major fighting.

Outcome: In the Treaty of Guadalupe Hidalgo, Mexico ceded more than 500,000 square miles (1.3 million km^2) to the U.S., including all or most of present-day California, Nevada, Arizona, Utah, and New Mexico and parts of five other states. The U.S. paid Mexico $15 million and all claims of U.S. citizens against Mexico.

around the neck of his horse and threw one leg over the saddle. Then, like a circus trick rider, he clung to the side of the horse and galloped through the streets, shielded from bullets by the body of his horse. He got the message through safely and, typically modest, gave more credit to his horse than to himself.

Grant received temporary promotions for bravery during the war, to first lieutenant and then to captain. The promotions were made permanent after the war was over. He also served as his regiment's *quartermaster*, the officer responsible for supplying troops with provisions, including food, clothing, and ammunition. He protested that he would rather be at the front "sharing in the dangers and honors of service," but he learned how important provisions were to an army. During the Civil War, he took great care to provide enough supplies for his troops. He also learned that he could do his job as quartermaster and still be involved in the fighting. When he heard the sound of battle, he headed for the front.

During the U.S.-Mexican War, Grant was involved in almost every major battle. He later wrote that when the fighting began, he was sorry that he had enlisted. It wasn't the danger that bothered him. In a letter to Julia he said, "There is no great sport in having bullets flying about one in every direction but I find they have less horror when among them than when in anticipation." He found, however, that he hated the destruction of war and the loss of human lives.

Grant as a young officer during the U.S.-Mexican War.

Resignation

After the war Grant returned to Missouri. He and Julia were married in August 1848, and he decided to remain in the army. She went with him to assignments in Detroit and Sackets Harbor, New York, on Lake Ontario. They made many friends at these bases, and in 1850, their first son, Fred, was born.

In the spring of 1852, Grant was ordered to duty on the Pacific Coast, at Fort Vancouver in present-day Washington State. When he received his orders, Julia was pregnant. Because travel to the Pacific Coast was very difficult in those days, Grant insisted that he go alone. He left Julia with his family in Ohio, where their second son, Ulysses Jr., was born. When the baby was old enough to travel, Julia went to Missouri and lived with her family. Grant hoped to save enough money to bring his family west to join him, but his army salary was small. Trying to make more, he lost the little he had saved in bad business ventures near the base. He could not afford to bring his family west, and he could not get a leave of several months to visit them.

Grant was reassigned to Fort Humboldt in northern California in 1854. In this isolated post, he spent some of the unhappiest days of his life. He missed Julia and his sons (one of whom he had never seen), and mail arrived only twice a month. He had few friends, and he did not get along with his superior officer. "You do not know how forsaken I feel here," he wrote to Julia. Finally, in April,

Grant was assigned to Fort Vancouver, in present-day Washington State, during the early 1850s.

Grant wrote a letter resigning his commission in the army. In May he began the long trip home, by ship to Panama, across the Isthmus of Panama on land, by ship to New York, and to St. Louis by rail.

In his *Memoirs*, Grant says that he resigned because he realized he could not support his wife and children. The gossip in the army was that Grant had been drinking to escape his depression. According to one story, he was found drunk during pay call and was given the choice of resigning or being *court-martialed*, brought before a military court to face charges of drunkenness. Rumors that he drank too much followed Grant through the rest of his career.

Life as a Civilian

In the fall of 1856, Ulysses and Julia Grant were together again with two small sons to care for. Julia's family had given the couple a parcel of undeveloped land near their own farm as a wedding gift. Grant decided to establish a farm there. He spent a year clearing the land and building a house. Privately, Julia thought the log home crude and homely, but Grant was proud of his handiwork. They named the house "Hardscrabble." Soon after they moved into the new house, Julia's mother died. It became clear that Julia's father needed help at White Haven, the family plantation. The Grants moved to White Haven early in 1858.

Grant managed both his own farm and his father-in-law's. He worked very hard, but money was scarce. He couldn't afford to buy all the seed and equipment he needed. Then, just when he finally harvested a good crop, prices fell. He was forced to auction off his own farm and equipment. In the next few years, he tried his hand at several businesses, but all of them failed. At one point, he was reduced to selling firewood on the streets of St. Louis.

In 1860 Grant was forced to ask his father for a job. By this time, Jesse owned several leather goods stores in northern Illinois. He offered Grant a job as a clerk at the store in the town of Galena. Grant would receive $600 a year and would work under the supervision of his two younger brothers. Grant became the billing clerk and collection agent. Once again, he proved to be a poor business-

Hardscrabble, the house that Grant built with his own hands in 1856 on land given to him by his father-in-law. The family lived there for a little more than a year.

man. He could not be tough with people who owed the firm money. If they told him a sad story, he would always give them more time to pay. Still, he used part of his salary to pay back all the money he had borrowed in Missouri, getting out of debt for the first time in years.

Chapter 2

Civil War

In 1860 Ulysses Grant seemed unlikely to be a great success in life. He was nearly 40 years old. Even with his West Point training, he had failed in the peacetime army. He had failed as a farmer and had lost thousands of dollars on poor business deals and investments. He now worked as a junior partner in the family business, reporting to his younger brothers. Yet in the remaining years of his life, he would become his country's most admired military leader and serve two terms as president.

The turning point in Grant's life was the beginning of the Civil War. In November 1860, Abraham Lincoln was elected president. He was the candidate of the new Republican party, which was opposed to the spread of slavery into the new territories in the West. Southern states, afraid that Republicans would limit or end slavery in the South, began to *secede* from the Union (withdraw from the United States). They organized the Confederate States of America and began to prepare for war. In April 1861, Confederate troops fired on Fort Sumter in Charleston, South Carolina, which was held by Union soldiers. President Lincoln issued a call for volunteers to fight to preserve the Union.

The citizens of Galena called on Grant to organize a rifle company for the coming war. It was a very small responsibility for a West Point graduate, but Grant organized and trained the volunteer unit. Then he marched them to Springfield, the state capital. There he volunteered his own services for the war effort. He met several officers he had known during the U.S.-Mexican War, but they seemed to have no army job for him. The rumor that he was a drunk persisted. Officers who had met him selling wood on St. Louis street corners were not willing to take a chance on him. These slights hurt him deeply.

Fortunately for Grant, Congressman Elihu Washburne, a resident of Galena, spoke up for his abilities. Washburne asked Illinois Governor Richard Yates to find a place for Grant as a commander of Illinois volunteers. Grant began to help organize the recruiting efforts in Springfield. One day, the 21st Illinois Infantry arrived. These volunteers were out of control. They stole food, got drunk, and ignored discipline. Their commander had quit in disgust. Governor Yates appointed Grant as their new colonel.

Grant quickly took control. He walked through the camp, observing the men and asking questions. He decided the problem lay with the officers and not with the enlisted men. He dismissed the troublemakers and dealt firmly with the rest. Within a few days, he achieved remarkable order. On July 3, 1861, the 21st Illinois marched proudly out of Springfield ready to go to war.

Now things finally began to go Grant's way. Before he was even in his first battle, Grant was promoted to brigadier general, thanks once again to Elihu Washburne. That fall he took part in the Union advance down the Mississippi. In November 1861, Grant led his men into their first battle, an attack on a Confederate camp in Belmont, Missouri. Grant lost about one-fifth of his men and had to retreat, but he gained valuable experience and the respect of his troops for his calm leadership.

In February 1862, Grant's troops, with the help of the U.S. Navy, sailed up the Ohio River into the Tennessee River, where they captured Fort Henry from the Confederates. Grant marched his men 12 miles (19 km) to the east and attacked Fort Donelson on the Cumberland River. When the Confederate commander sent out a message asking for terms of surrender, Grant replied that he would accept nothing less than "unconditional and immediate surrender." From that day on, his troops insisted that his initials stood for "Unconditional Surrender."

HARPER'S WEEKLY.
A JOURNAL OF CIVILIZATION.

VOL. VI.—No. 270.]   NEW YORK, SATURDAY, MARCH 1, 1862.   [SINGLE COPIES SIX CENTS. [$2 50 PER YEAR IN ADVANCE.

Entered according to Act of Congress, in the Year 1862, by Harper & Brothers, in the Clerk's Office of the District Court for the Southern District of New York.

THE SURRENDER OF FORT DONELSON, FEBRUARY 16, 1862.—[See Next Page.]

Confederates at Fort Donelson wave a flag of truce, ending the battle. Grant gained his nickname, "Unconditional Surrender" Grant after this battle.

The victories at Forts Henry and Donelson were the first major successes for any Union army and made Grant's name familiar throughout the Union. The loss of the forts forced the Confederacy to give up western Kentucky and middle Tennessee, including Nashville, the state capital.

Grant Takes Charge in the West

In April 1862, Grant's command in western Tennessee was tested by a surprise Confederate attack near the old Shiloh Meeting House (a church). On the first day, Grant's army was driven back and almost defeated. Grant remained cool and controlled, however. The following morning, supported by fresh reinforcements, the Union fighters drove the Confederates from the field and forced them to retreat southward into Mississippi. More than 100,000 men participated in the battle, which was the largest in the war up to that time.

As Grant's talents as a battlefield leader began to show themselves, he gained wider command over Union armies in the western theater of the war. He quarreled with some of his superiors, but his greatest supporter was President Lincoln. Many of Lincoln's generals were so cautious that they preferred to wait for Confederate attacks. By contrast, Grant was willing to take the battle to the enemy.

Through the winter of 1862–63, Grant directed a Union campaign against Vicksburg, Mississippi. This fortress city stood on high bluffs overlooking the

Mississippi River, where it could fire on any Union ships traveling upstream or down. After many fruitless attacks, Grant decided to float his army downstream under the guns of Vicksburg at night and land them south of the city. This daring action was successful. His troops marched around the city and cut off its supplies of food and ammunition. By late May, the city was *besieged*, or surrounded by enemy troops. Finally, with townspeople and troops near starvation, Vicksburg surrendered on July 4, 1863. Nearly 30,000 Confederate soldiers were taken

Unable to attack Vicksburg from the north, Grant moved his troops down the Mississippi River at night past the city's powerful defenses. He landed south of the city and captured it after a long siege.

prisoner. Together with a great victory at Gettysburg, Pennsylvania, only one day earlier, Vicksburg helped turn the tide of war in favor of the Union.

Later that year, Grant traveled eastward to the outskirts of Chattanooga, Tennessee, near the Georgia-Tennessee border. There a Confederate army had trapped a Union force and threatened to force its surrender. Grant found a new supply route to keep the troops in Chattanooga from starving. Then late in November, Union forces attacked strong Confederate positions on Missionary Ridge and Lookout Mountain to the east and south of the city. In three days of fighting, the Confederate lines were broken, and they retreated eastward into Georgia in another major Union victory.

Grant Takes Command in the East

His successes in the western battles would have made Grant one of the great heroes of the war. However, the war in the eastern theater was going poorly. After the great victory at Gettysburg, Union forces were unable to drive the Confederate armies out of northern Virginia. The people of the North were war-weary, and some wanted to stop the fighting and negotiate a settlement with the Confederates.

In March 1864, President Lincoln called Grant to Washington and appointed him supreme commander of all Union forces. He wanted Grant to take charge of the Union armies in Virginia and to plan an overall strategy to end the war quickly. Grant left his trusted colleague, General William T. Sherman, in command of Union forces outside of Chattanooga with orders to drive the Confederate army there back toward Atlanta, the capital of Georgia. Grant himself took command of the army in northern Virginia.

In May, Grant and his armies were on the march. They first clashed with General Robert E. Lee's Confederates in the region known as the Wilderness, near Chancellorsville, Virginia. In three days of desperate fighting, both armies suffered huge casualties. Other Union generals would have retreated, but Grant was different. He moved his army sideways, to the east and south toward

An Ordinary Man

Nearly everyone who knew Grant described him as *unpretentious*. He was a humble, plain man, not interested in trying to make himself seem important. When he arrived in Washington, D.C., in March 1864 to assume command of the Union armies, he was dressed in his usual shabby fashion, accompanied only by his 13-year-old son, Frederick. Grant walked into the Willard Hotel and asked for a room. The desk clerk looked him over and said they might have a small room available on the top floor. Grant agreed. When he signed the guest register "U. S. Grant and son, Galena, Illinois," the desk clerk suddenly showed new respect for his guest. He discovered that the best suite in the hotel was available. Grant said that would be fine, too. Really, any room would do.

☆ ☆ ☆

Grant at ease during his campaign against Robert E. Lee's army in 1864.

Robert E. Lee

Robert E. Lee (1807–1870) was a Virginian. Fifteen years older than Ulysses S. Grant, he graduated second in his class at West Point in 1829, where he was the first cadet in its history to graduate without a single demerit. After serving in the U.S.-Mexican War, he became superintendent at West Point and later a cavalry colonel. When the Civil War broke out, President Lincoln offered Lee the field command of the Union army, but he declined, saying that he could not lead an attack against his home state.

After Virginia seceded from the Union, Lee resigned from the U.S. Army and became a military adviser to Confederate president Jefferson Davis. A year later he was given command of the Army of Northern Virginia. He was a brilliant military leader who took daring chances to defeat armies larger and better equipped than his own. Even in defeat, he became one of the most admired generals of the Civil War.

☆ ★ ☆

Richmond. Lee was forced to move with him. In the next few weeks, the two great armies met again at Spotsylvania, North Anna, and Cold Harbor. Each time, the losses on both sides were huge, but Grant was wearing down the Confederate army and moving closer to Richmond. From Spotsylvania, he wrote to Lincoln, "I will fight it out on this line if it takes all summer."

Soon afterward, Grant was forced to change his strategy. After heavy losses at Cold Harbor, he decided to slip all the way around Lee's army to the east and south. There he could attack the important railroad junction at Petersburg, south of Richmond. The capital's food and ammunition came through Petersburg. If Grant could capture the city, the Confederate government and troops in Richmond would have to flee. By mid-June 1864, Union troops had surrounded Petersburg, but they were not able to capture it. For nine long months, the armies skirmished, but neither was willing to give up.

In the meantime, General Sherman drove the stubborn Confederate armies in Georgia back toward Atlanta. By late summer, he was closing in. Finally, the city surrendered on September 2, 1864. The Confederate army retreated northward into the mountains. Sherman decided not to follow them. With most of his troops, he left Atlanta in November and set out to the east. Meeting little resistance, he marched from Atlanta to Savannah, Georgia, on the Atlantic coast, capturing that city on December 24.

War's End

By the end of 1864, the Confederacy had been cut in pieces. The Union controlled the Mississippi River, isolating the Confederate states of Texas, Louisiana, and Arkansas to the west. Sherman's march across Georgia had cut off communication with regions to the south. The Confederacy was running out of soldiers, ammunition, and food. Grant, Sherman, and other Union commanders had done their work well, and the war was nearly over.

Who: The United States (the Union, or the North) against the Confederate States of America (the South), made up of southern states that had seceded from the Union

When: April 12, 1861–May 1865

Why: Southern states, believing the election of Abraham Lincoln threatened states' rights and slavery, seceded from the United States and fought for their independence. The North fought to restore the southern states to the Union, and later to end slavery.

Where: States along the border between the Union and the Confederacy, especially Virginia and Tennessee. Confederate forces had some early successes, but were overcome by the Union's superior resources. Major northern victories came at Gettysburg, Pennsylvania, and Vicksburg, Mississippi (both July 1863); Atlanta, Georgia (September 1864); and Petersburg and Richmond, Virginia (both April 1865).

Outcome: The Confederate Army of Northern Virginia surrendered to Union forces April 9, 1865, ending the major fighting. The victorious North passed legislation that abolished slavery, gave civil rights to former slaves, and put defeated states under military rule. Efforts to reconstruct the South continued until 1877.

As spring arrived in 1865, General Sherman marched north through the Carolinas. The Confederate army was so weak that it could not offer strong resistance. Grant made a final attack on Confederate defenders of Petersburg, finally breaking through their defenses on April 2. This forced the Confederate government and its troops to evacuate Richmond, retreating to the west.

On April 9, Lee sent a message to Grant asking for a meeting to discuss the surrender of his army. They met at Appomattox Court House, Virginia. Grant offered generous surrender terms. The soldiers would be allowed to return to their homes if they turned in their weapons and promised never again to take up arms against the federal government. Officers would even be allowed to keep their personal sidearms and horses. The surrender ceremony was held two days later. Recalling

Grant and General Robert E. Lee shake hands after the Confederate surrender at Appomattox Courthouse, Virginia, in April 1865.

that day, Grant wrote, "I felt like anything rather than rejoicing at the downfall of a foe who had fought so long and valiantly, and had suffered so much for a cause, though that cause was, I believe, one of the worst for which a people ever fought, and one for which there was the least excuse."

Tragedy Strikes

On April 13, Grant returned to Washington, D.C., where he received a hero's welcome. On Friday, April 14, he attended a cabinet meeting at the White House. Afterward, President Lincoln invited the Grants to join him and Mrs. Lincoln at the

General of the Army Ulysses S. Grant.

theater that evening. At first, Grant accepted, but Julia persuaded him to change his mind so that they could set out to visit their children in New Jersey. At Ford's Theatre that evening, President Lincoln was shot by the assassin John Wilkes Booth. He died the next morning. For the rest of his life, Grant regretted his decision not to go to the theater. He believed that if he had been there, he might have prevented the assassination. Julia, however, believed that if Grant had been there, he would have been killed, too.

Grant and Lincoln had formed a close working relationship during the war. During the siege of Petersburg, Lincoln visited Grant's headquarters several times to discuss strategy. Only weeks before the assassination, the two had met with General Sherman and others to talk about the coming end of the war and to plan for peace. Grant continued to serve with the title General of the Army until 1869, but he would sadly miss his first commander in chief.

Serving Under President Johnson ———

After Lincoln's death, Vice President Andrew Johnson was sworn in as president. Johnson had been chosen because he was a Democrat and a southerner who had remained loyal to the Union even after his state of Tennessee seceded. Johnson favored the abolition of slavery and believed that the leaders of the Confederacy should be punished. On the other hand, he believed that the federal government should make it easy for the states of the South to rejoin the Union and send new representatives to Washington.

Congress was controlled by Radical Republicans who believed the southern states should be dealt with more strictly. They believed that freedmen (former slaves) should be declared citizens with full civil rights, including the right to vote. They favored military rule in the former Confederate states until the states could meet strict requirements for rejoining the Union.

It soon became clear that President Johnson and Congress were on a collision course. Congress passed laws for strict "reconstruction" of the South, and Johnson *vetoed* them (refused to sign them into law). He condemned congressional leaders, using harsh language. Congress passed the Reconstruction laws by *overriding* Johnson's veto (by passing them with two-thirds majorities in both the House and the Senate). They also began to restrict the president's power to appoint high officials. In 1867, Johnson defied these restrictions by suspending Edwin Stanton, his secretary of war, and asking General Grant to serve in his place.

This bitter conflict between the president and Congress put General Grant in a difficult position. As a military professional, Grant had always tried to stay out of politics. According to the Constitution, the president is the nation's military commander in chief, and even the General of the Army is required to follow his orders. Grant reluctantly agreed to serve temporarily as secretary of war.

Early in 1868, Congress ordered the president to restore Edwin Stanton as secretary of war. Grant resigned and Stanton took over his duties once again. President Johnson harshly denounced Congress. To threaten them, he began working to form a new army unit in Washington under his command. At this point, Grant withdrew his support of Johnson and began to work with leaders of Congress. Johnson responded by accusing Grant of disloyalty to his country.

In March 1868, Johnson fired Edwin Stanton and replaced him with a new appointee. Days afterward, the House of Representatives voted to *impeach* Johnson, bringing formal charges against him. In April and May, Johnson was tried on the charges, with the U.S. Senate sitting as the jury. When the Senate voted, it failed by one vote to convict Johnson and remove him from office. Still, the president was discredited, and he remained powerless throughout his remaining months in office.

The Election of 1868

As the election of 1868 approached, Republicans began to rally around Grant as their next presidential candidate. He claimed that he did not really want the job, yet he did not refuse to be considered. In May, the Republican party convention nominated him on the first ballot. In his written acceptance, he concluded with the words, "Let us have peace," which would be the theme of the campaign. The Democratic party nominated Horatio Seymour of New York.

In November, Grant won. He received about 3.0 million votes to Seymour's 2.7 million, and carried 26 of 34 states in the electoral college. His election was assured by the votes of the southern states, which were admitted to the Union just in time for the election. In much of the South, former slaves, voting in a presidential election for the first time, outnumbered white voters. Under the protection of

The festive inauguration ceremonies for Grant in 1869. For the first time, the Capitol is bedecked with American flags.

Republican-controlled military governments, nearly all of them cast their votes for Grant.

What Kind of President?

Many of Grant's supporters were attracted to him because he was not a politician. During his military career, he was careful to avoid politics, and during his years in civilian life, he had little time or interest to devote to political activities. In fact, he announced that he was a Republican less than a year before the Republicans nominated him. Grant had never run for a political office.

Being nonpolitical would prove to be Grant's greatest strength as president. He owed very little to political factions in Congress or in the country. He was admired both by Radical Republicans and by conservatives in both parties. This gave him the freedom to follow his own vision for improving and developing the nation.

Yet Grant's lack of political experience also proved to be his greatest weakness. As a military man, he was used to a world in which he obeyed the orders of his superior officers and expected his orders to be obeyed by lesser officers. As president, he had to work in a more complicated world. Politicians in Congress and in the states expected him to compromise and to be more sensitive to the opinions of others, including the newspapers and the general public.

Grant got off to a bad start when he announced the names of his new cabinet officers. He had not consulted Republican leaders in Congress and had not tried to balance his cabinet between different political factions. Like a military commander, he appointed men who seemed to be able and whom he could work with. The public was enthusiastic about his appointments. The U.S. Senate was less happy. Senators were insulted that Grant had not asked their opinion and disappointed that qualified candidates they supported had not been appointed. To teach Grant a lesson, they pointed out that his choice for secretary of the treasury, Alexander Stewart, was not eligible by law. They forced Stewart to resign, and Grant appointed another candidate. This was the first of many difficulties Grant would face with Congress.

Reconstruction

The most pressing task facing the government was Reconstruction—restoring peace between the North and South while protecting the rights of newly freed African Americans. At the end of the Civil War, Grant had agreed with Lincoln that southern states should be admitted back into the Union on easy terms as soon as possible. Since then, however, conditions had changed. Congress had passed a much more demanding Reconstruction program. Before Grant was elected, it had sent northern military units into the South and set up new state governments controlled by Republicans and elected by the voting power of freedmen. Nearly all freedmen voted for Republican candidates.

Grant had come to agree with the Republicans in Congress that southern states must give full rights to freedmen. Weeks before his inauguration Congress had passed the Fifteenth Amendment to the Constitution, which guaranteed African American men the right to vote. Grant supported the amendment, believing that with the power to vote, freedmen would be able to protect their other civil

Grant and African Americans

Grant's attitude toward slavery and African Americans was full of contradiction. His parents were strongly against slavery, and Grant learned to oppose it. However, Julia's family, the Dents, owned slaves, and Julia's father strongly defended slavery. Grant did not try to change them. When the Grants lived in Missouri, Julia's father gave her several slaves, who helped run the household and take care of the children. When Colonel Dent gave Grant a slave in 1859, Grant freed the man, even though he was broke at the time and could have used the money he would have gotten by selling him.

During the Civil War, Grant's ideas changed gradually. At Lincoln's urging, he supported recruiting African American soldiers to fight for the Union and came to respect their abilities. By the time he was elected president in 1869, Grant was an outspoken supporter of full civil rights for African Americans. When southern whites refused to allow African Americans to vote or hold office, he sent in federal troops to protect them.

☆ ☆ ☆

rights. In his inaugural address, he urged the states to *ratify*, or officially approve, the amendment. Just over a year later, the amendment became effective when it was ratified by three-fourths of the states.

In the meantime, it was becoming clear that simple words on paper would not assure the rights of African Americans. As they voted for the first time in 1867 and 1868, southern whites resorted to terrorism to keep them away from the polls. The Ku Klux Klan and other secret societies sent out night riders, disguised by

Grant supported giving African Americans the right to vote, and during his presidency, many of them did (above). This stirred up a powerful backlash among whites in the South. At right, a white southerner threatens an African American, but a federal soldier restrains him.

masks made of white sheets, to frighten African Americans and whites suspected of favoring Republicans. They committed arson, assault, and murder in the name of white supremacy. Local authorities looked the other way.

With Grant's support, Congress passed new laws making it a federal crime to deny civil rights to people of any race. Grant sent army units to places where violence and terrorism were widespread. Nearly a thousand violators were arrested and more than half were convicted of federal crimes. To handle the additional activity in federal courts, Congress created the Department of Justice. Yet the violence continued and hundreds of cases of arson and murder went unsolved.

On March 4, 1871, Grant asked Congress for special laws to help end the power of the Ku Klux Klan. It allowed the federal government to use the army to pursue and prosecute Klan members who killed African Americans, burned their houses, and terrorized them. When the bill faced strong opposition in Congress, Grant made a personal appeal, putting all the power of his popularity and his office behind the bill. It finally passed April 20, 1871. Grant appealed to citizens of the South to help end the violence. When it continued, he sent in troops and finally succeeded in breaking up the Klan. In the elections of 1872, a larger percentage of African Americans voted than in any presidential election until the 1960s. Ulysses S. Grant easily won his second term in office.

The Ku Klux Klan published the cartoon above to intimidate "scalawags" (African Americans who voted) and "carpetbaggers" (whites from the North who helped organize the black vote). In response, Grant supported and signed the Ku Klux Klan Act (below), which gave federal authorities power to prosecute the group.

The Gold Scandal

Early in Grant's first term, two wealthy investors hatched a plan to gain control of New York's gold market. James Fisk and Jay Gould had made millions investing in railroads, and now they saw a chance to get even richer. Their plans depended on gaining inside information about when the U.S. government would be selling gold and how much it planned to sell. Using that information, they could buy huge amounts of gold and cause the price per ounce to skyrocket. Later, they could sell the gold for a huge profit.

One way they tried to gain inside information was to make friends with Abel Corbin, a wealthy New York businessman who was married to Grant's sister. They persuaded him that increased gold prices would be good for the country and got him to invest some of his money. Through Corbin, Fisk and Gould met and entertained Grant and Julia when they visited New York.

In the late summer of 1869, the two men began buying large quantities of gold. The price began to rise steeply. By September 6, the price had risen to $137 an ounce. A few weeks later, Fisk and Gould convinced Corbin to send a letter to President Grant, urging him to stop selling the government's gold, which would send the price even higher. When Grant read the letter, he realized that Fisk and Gould were behind it and that that they were responsible for rapidly rising gold prices. He ordered his secretary of the treasury to offer $4 million worth of gold for sale. With so much gold for sale, the price per ounce was sure to drop.

The government sale was announced on September 24, which came to be known as Black Friday. The price of gold fell from $162 to $133 in a few minutes. The sale ruined the illegal plan of Fisk and Gould, but it also ruined hundreds of smaller investors, who were hoping to make a profit. The sudden drop of gold prices caused a panic among other investors as well, and the country seemed headed for a depression. Much of the suspicion fell on Grant. Investors knew that his brother-in-law was a friend of Jim Fisk and Jay Gould, and that the president had been seen with them in New York.

Further investigation showed that Grant had no knowledge of the plot, and that Abel Corbin had been deceived into helping Fisk and Gould. In fact, Grant had acted quickly to help stabilize the market and end the scheme. Still, Grant's association with the illegal scheme damaged his reputation. It was only the first of many scandals to hurt his presidency.

The Treaty of Washington

In foreign affairs, the Grant administration scored a big success during his first term. During the Civil War, Great Britain quietly gave help to the Confederacy.

Grant could be decisive and courageous in war and in politics. Yet Julia Grant was one person he could not stand up against. Throughout their marriage it was clear she adored Grant and was always fiercely loyal to him, but she was not submissive or meek, and she knew how to get her own way. She frequently joined Grant wherever he was headquartered and didn't hesitate to offer her opinion on any topic.

Grant and Julia with their daughter and three sons at the White House.

Once during the Civil War, a woman carrying a baby approached Julia just after she'd left Grant asleep in their room. The woman pleaded to see General Grant. Julia refused at first, but the woman explained frantically that she had persuaded her husband to sneak away from the army to come home to see the baby and that now he was to be shot that very day as a deserter.

Julia woke her husband up and told him the story. He insisted that he wouldn't see the woman and that he couldn't interfere in a decision made by the man's commanding officer. Julia brought the woman into his room anyway. Grant listened to her and agreed to pardon the man. After the woman left, Grant said to Julia, "I'm sure I did wrong. I've no doubt I have pardoned a bounty jumper who ought to have been hanged."

But he couldn't say "no" to Julia.

Three warships built by Great Britain for use by the Confederate States had done great damage to Union shipping. Congress was demanding an apology and money to cover the damages. In late 1870, the British government offered to negotiate the claims. Grant's secretary of state, Hamilton Fish, carried on several months of difficult negotiation with the British. The two countries produced what one historian called "a landmark of international *conciliation*," each side giving a little to bring them together. In the treaty, Great Britain expressed regret for the damage the ships had done, agreed to submit the damage claims to a board of arbitration, and agreed to pay the amount of damages determined by the board. The treaty also set up new rules for a nation which wishes to stay neutral during a war between other countries.

The Election of 1872

The Grants were ready and eager to remain in the White House for four more years. Grant believed there was much work left to be done and was committed to completing it. Julia had come to enjoy her position as first lady and was happy to continue.

Others were not so eager to reelect Grant, however. A group of Republicans from the Northeast were increasingly unhappy with the government's policies in the South. They were especially outraged by the actions of the U.S. army in the South. It was time, they said, to end these police actions, leave law enforcement to the states, and make a lasting peace with the South. Many left the Republican party and formed the Liberal Republican party. They met and nominated the distinguished newspaper editor Horace Greeley for president. The Democrats decided to cooperate with the Liberal Republicans, and they also nominated Greeley.

For a time, the opposition seemed to be gaining ground on the president and the Republicans. The more people heard, however, the less they liked the idea of withdrawing from the South. They doubted the southern states could be trusted to treat African Americans fairly. Worse yet, the elderly Horace Greeley was not an appealing candidate. The Liberals' claims that Grant's administration was corrupt had some truth, but Grant himself was more popular than ever.

Grant won the election by a landslide. Grant began his second term in office with optimism and confidence. Only gradually did it become clear that events beyond his control and scandals within the government would make his final four years a misery.

A Peace Policy with the American Indians ——

Four years earlier, Grant had begun as president determined to find a new and better policy for dealing with American Indians. He felt that they had been treated cruelly by settlers and by the government in past years. In a message to Congress and the American people in January 1869, he proposed a new peace policy. He stated bluntly, "Our dealings with the Indian properly lay us open to charges of cruelty and swindling." Soon afterward he appointed a Seneca Indian, Ely S. Parker, as commissioner of Indian affairs.

The States During the Presidency of Ulysses S. Grant

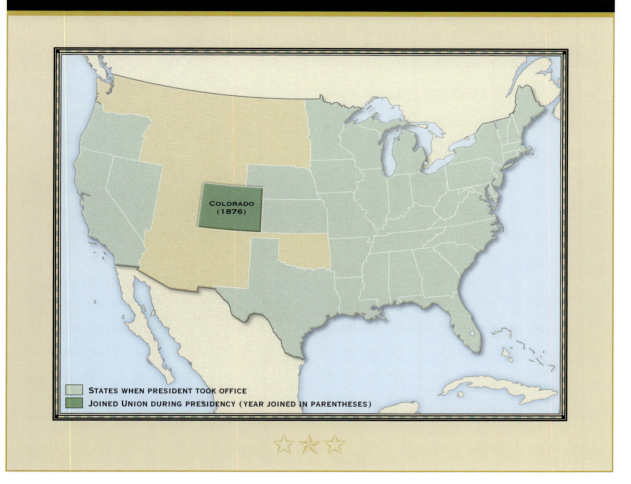

COLORADO
(1876)

STATES WHEN PRESIDENT TOOK OFFICE

JOINED UNION DURING PRESIDENCY (YEAR JOINED IN PARENTHESES)

Ely S. Parker

Ely S. Parker (1828–1895) was born Ha-sa-no-an-da on the Senecas' Tonawanda Reservation in western New York and went to a Baptist mission school, where he took the name Ely Parker. He studied law and civil engineering and became a translator for his Indian nation with the U.S. government. He became chief of the Senecas and grand sachem, or chief, of the six Iroquois nations. In 1860, he was serving as an engineer for the U.S. government in Galena, Illinois, when he met Ulysses S. Grant. During the Civil War he served as a captain of engineers in the Union army. After the battle of Vicksburg in 1863, he became an officer on Grant's staff and in 1864, Grant appointed him his military secretary. At Appomattox, Ely Parker wrote the final copy of the surrender that Lee and Grant signed.

Grant appointed Ely Parker, a Native American, to be in charge of the federal Bureau of Indian Affairs. It was part of a plan to deal more fairly and gently with Native Americans.

After the war, Parker became an adviser to Grant in Washington. In 1869 Grant appointed him his first commissioner of Indian affairs. Some American Indians viewed Parker as a traitor because he believed American Indians should become part of white culture. Parker resigned as commissioner in 1871, after he was accused of misconduct in awarding government contracts. A congressional investigation cleared him of all charges, but he never worked in the federal government again. He settled in New York City, where he became a businessman, and later worked for the city's police board of commissioners. He died in 1895.

☆ ★ ☆

In his second annual report to Congress in 1870, Grant outlined his "Peace Policy" for dealing with American Indians on the frontier. He believed that Indians, like the freedmen in the South, should prepare to become citizens of the United States. He proposed that they settle in reservations, where the federal Indian Bureau could teach them farming technique and introduce them to Christianity. This peaceful policy would represent a sharp change of direction for the government.

Until Grant's time, government management of American Indians was often carried out by corrupt Indian agents and by the U.S. army, which saw its main job as protecting white settlers against Indian attack. Grant proposed to replace the corrupt agents with Quakers and members of other religious organizations, who could be trusted to deal more fairly with the Indians. He also appointed a commission to study the condition of American Indians and recommend improvements in their treatment.

As Grant entered his second term, the peace policy had made some progress. However, western delegates to Congress, railroad owners, and settlers along the frontier continued to oppose it bitterly. They wanted the American Indians out of their way. Three weeks after Grant's reelection, a group of Modoc Indians left their reservation and attempted to return to their former home in northern California. Army troops failed to round them up and return them to the reservation. Grant ordered the military leadership to stop fighting the Modoc and to begin negotiations. The meetings were long and difficult. Then on April 11, 1873, the Modoc negotiators pulled out guns and opened fire on government negotiators, killing several, including an army general and a Methodist minister. Public opinion turned against American Indians. Opponents of Grant's peace policy demanded tougher policies.

Violence broke out between American Indians and settlers in other places over the next two years. In 1874 gold was discovered in the Black Hills of the Dakota Territory. As word of the discovery spread, white gold prospectors flocked to the area, even though it was in Sioux territory. The army couldn't stop the prospectors. The Grant administration offered to buy the Black Hills, but the Sioux considered it a sacred place and refused the offer.

Troubled by reports of violence, Grant finally agreed with General Philip Sheridan that the Sioux should be rounded up and forced onto a reservation outside the Black Hills. Sheridan sent three army units to accomplish this. One, commanded by General George Armstrong Custer, attacked an American Indian encampment near the Little Bighorn River on June 25, 1876. The Sioux, waiting in ambush, surrounded Custer's troops and killed nearly every soldier.

Even though Custer had made a foolhardy attack, the nation was shocked by the massacre. Throughout the West, volunteers arrived at military bases, ready

The massacre of General George Custer's troops by Sioux warriors in 1876 created a backlash against Grant's gentler policies. This picture of the battle was made by a Sioux artist.

to avenge Custer's defeat. Grant reluctantly gave General Sheridan permission to do whatever was necessary to force the Sioux onto the reservation. Although Grant continued to speak for his peace policy, many now considered it a failure, and Congress was no longer willing to support him.

Retreat in the South

The struggle in the South continued into Grant's second term as well. White southerners refused to grant full rights to African Americans. Republicans and black voters were still being terrorized. In Colfax, Louisiana, whites refused to accept the results of a state election that chose Republican officeholders, including African Americans. They stormed the courthouse and set the building on fire. More than a hundred African Americans were killed, some after surrendering. Only two whites were killed. No one went to jail.

In September 1874, a group of Democrats calling themselves the White League seized the statehouse in New Orleans and installed their own government. Grant sent 5,000 troops, under the command of General Sheridan, to restore

Even with federal troops in the South, the persecution of African Americans continued. Many disappeared and their bodies were found days or weeks later in a river.

order. This outraged the public, North and South, who felt Grant was overstepping his authority as president. On January 4, 1875, White Leaguers again attempted to install their own government in New Orleans. Sheridan had them forcibly removed and asked Grant's permission to treat them like bandits. Again the press and the public were outraged, claiming that Grant was "riding roughshod over the Bill of Rights."

Nearly ten years after the Civil War, the public was tired of the battles in the South. It seemed that little progress had been made in creating a reconstructed South, and the federal government was spending millions of dollars to police citizens of southern states. A few months later, violence broke out in Mississippi. The governor asked Grant to send federal troops. This time, Grant refused. The long struggle to reconstruct the South was coming to an end.

The Panic of 1873

As Grant started his second term, the economy seemed strong, but there were danger signs. In the years after the Civil War, railroads had built thousands of miles of new track, competing fiercely with each other for government support and for business. Railroads had borrowed huge sums from banks to finance their new construction. It became clear that some railroads had borrowed money for lines that would never make a profit. When they weren't able to repay the loans,

In the panic of 1873, businessmen wait outside a bank to withdraw their funds. Hundreds of banks went out of business, and their depositors lost their money.

the banks began to declare bankruptcy. Jay Cooke and Company, one of the biggest, closed its doors on September 18, 1873. Railroad stocks began to fall, and investors panicked. On September 20, the stock market crashed, and all trading was stopped for ten days. Within months, 89 of the nation's 364 railroads went out of business. The effects rippled through the economy. Prices fell, and a startling 18,000 businesses collapsed. A severe depression hit the nation. By 1876, unemployment had risen to 14 percent.

Grant knew what it was like to be broke and unable to support a family. He sympathized with those who were suffering, yet there was little he could do. Some urged him to release more paper money, even if the government couldn't back it with gold. They said this could help small businesses and farmers. Grant's advisers warned him, however, that the policy would quickly lead to rising prices, causing even more damage to the economy. Congress passed a bill to release $100 million in paper money. Grant vetoed the bill, causing many voters to blame him personally for the continuing hard times.

Scandals

Even as Grant faced trouble with American Indians, violence in the South, and a major depression, his worst problems came from within his own administration. Grant had a long history of trusting the wrong people, and now he would begin to pay for this failing.

One of Grant's early programs was designed to improve the collection of taxes. The Treasury Department hired many new collection agents to pursue businesses and rich individuals who were not paying. Agents were allowed to keep half of all the money they collected and could soon become rich. There was so much abuse in this system that Congress passed a law ending the collection program in 1872. However, Congressman Benjamin Butler of Massachusetts, a leading

Congressman Benjamin Butler was one of Grant's allies accused of profiting from government corruption.

Republican and a supporter of Grant, managed to add an exception to the law. It allowed one of his supporters, John D. Sanborn, to continue as an agent. Treasury officials referred Sanborn to overdue accounts, then he collected them and took half the money, receiving more than $200,000 (then a huge fortune). An investigation revealed that Sanborn may have shared the money with Grant's secretary of the treasury and with Congressman Butler. Grant publicly defended his secretary of the treasury, but in the end, the secretary was forced to resign.

In 1874, it was discovered that companies that made and sold alcoholic beverages were avoiding federal taxes by bribing tax collectors. Investigators discovered that this so-called Whiskey Ring had cheated the government out of $4 million in taxes. Among the 350 people brought to trial were two close friends of Grant. His personal secretary, Orville Babcock, was forced to resign,

Personally, Grant was honest to a fault. He was once stopped by a policeman in Washington for driving his carriage too fast. When the officer realized he had stopped the president, he offered to let him go. Grant insisted that the man give him a summons, and he paid the fine.

★ ★ ☆

and his friend, General John McDonald of St. Louis, was convicted of charges and went to jail.

With each new scandal, Grant's reputation suffered. No one accused him of taking illegal payments or personally breaking the law. Yet those accused were men he had personally appointed. He seemed blind to the possibility that they could corrupt the government. Grant had never been one to shirk responsibility. In his final address to Congress, he admitted that "mistakes have been made," and apologized.

Despite all the scandals Grant's personal popularity remained high. Even though he was worn out by the stress of eight years in the White House, he was tempted to run for a third term, something no president had ever done. At the Republican convention in 1876, however, the party decided it was time for a new candidate. They nominated Rutherford B. Hayes of Ohio, hoping he would be able to end the long string of scandals that had so damaged Grant's last term.

A Contested Election

Before he left office, Grant learned how much damage had been done to the Republican party. It had won every presidential election since 1860, but in 1876 its prospects were not bright. Rutherford B. Hayes, the Republican candidate, and Samuel Tilden, his Democratic opponent, both ran on pledges to "clean up the mess in Washington." Many voters believed that the first step was to sweep the Republicans out and let a Democrat have a chance.

The presidential election in November was one of the closest in history, and it ended with a contested result. Tilden, the Democrat, won more popular votes. It appeared that he had also won more electoral votes and gained election. There were disputed returns in four states, however. Only if Hayes won all four of the states could he be elected.

The election was thrown into the House of Representatives, which was unable to make a decision. Finally it established the Electoral Commission, made up of five Supreme Court justices, five representatives, and five senators. Seven of the members were Democrats, and eight were Republicans. Finally in March 1877, only three days before the scheduled inauguration, the commission decided by votes of eight to seven that Hayes had won all four disputed states and was elected president.

Democrats on the Electoral Commission agreed that they would not protest the election of Hayes if the new administration would agree to change its policy in the South. Democrats wanted an end to the long military occupation, leaving southern states to police themselves. The Republican negotiators agreed. This was the final retreat in the battle to establish civil rights and voting rights for African Americans. Within a year, southern states withdrew many of these rights. New state laws made it difficult for African Americans to vote or to exercise many other rights enjoyed by white citizens. A new battle for civil rights would not begin for 75 years.

Rutherford B. Hayes, who won the disputed election of 1876 and followed Grant to the presidency.

On inauguration day, Grant was relieved to welcome another Republican to the presidency, but he must have regretted the retreat in the South. However much he had wanted a third term, he wrote that when he left the White House, he "felt like a boy getting out of school."

Chapter 5

A World Tour

Grant was only 54 years old when he left office. He was unemployed once again, but now, for the first time in his life, he had a little money. He had invested in a silver mine in Nevada, which had struck a huge vein of silver. Grant's share was worth about $25,000. He and Julia decided to use the money to do some traveling.

In May 1877, Grant and Julia, with their youngest son, Jesse, and two servants boarded a ship to England with no set plans in mind. John Russell Young, a reporter for the *New York Herald*, also accompanied them. Grant said that they planned to travel until the money ran out. They were traveling as private citizens and did not expect a formal reception when they arrived. Yet when they docked in Liverpool, England, they were met by a huge, cheering crowd and the mayor of the city. Wherever they went, crowds gathered to greet them. They dined with dukes and duchesses and were presented at court. In London, Grant was given the freedom of the city, the highest honor that city could offer, and the couple dined at Windsor Castle with Queen Victoria. The Grants spent some time with their daughter, Nellie, who had married an Englishman, and then moved on. For two and a half years, they wandered through Europe, North Africa, and Asia.

Retired president Grant and his wife (right-center) are introduced to Queen Victoria of Great Britain (left-center) during their world tour in 1877.

A Shopping Trip

During the trip, Julia shopped almost without stopping. In Paris, just before Christmas, the Grants visited a famous jewelry store. A jeweled butterfly caught Julia's eye. Its body was a topaz, its wings diamonds, and its eyes bright rubies. When Julia learned what it cost, she turned away, but she kept thinking of it. Soon, she convinced herself that it wasn't that expensive. After all, she could wear it in her hair, replacing the flowers and feathers she bought all the time. Grant had watched her struggle with amusement and told her they really had to leave.

Outside, Julia turned back, intending to buy the butterfly. Grant reminded her that he never turned back once he had a goal. Julia wasn't happy, but she went with him. On Christmas morning, the butterfly was sitting at Julia's place at the breakfast table.

☆☆☆

The Grants were awed by some of the sights they saw. They viewed masterpieces of art in major museums and visited places of great natural beauty. They saw the pyramids of Egypt, the ancient ruins in Athens, and the sites sacred to Christianity in the Holy Land. Gifts poured in. Grant's favorite came from the sultan of Turkey, who gave him two purebred Arabian horses. John Young sent articles back to his newspaper, describing the Grants' adventures. Citizens in the United States followed these travel accounts eagerly and felt proud of the reception Grant received.

Former first lady Julia Grant.

Finally in September 1879, the Grants left Tokyo to return to the United States. They received a 21-gun salute while a crowd waved American and Japanese flags and a band played "Hail Columbia." They were welcomed to San Francisco in an equally enthusiastic manner. They proceeded to tour the country as they had been touring the world, traveling, as Julia put it, "from east to west, from north to south." Everywhere crowds greeted and cheered them. Finally, they settled in Galena, Illinois, in the house the town had given them at the close of the Civil War.

Failure Again

When Grant returned to Galena, it seemed he might not have to look for a job. There was strong support for his nomination to run again for the presidency in 1880. Grant was interested, but he refused to campaign personally. For 35 ballots, Grant led in the race for the nomination, but he never gained a majority. He might have tipped the balance by making a personal appearance, but he refused. Finally the exhausted delegates rallied behind a dark-horse candidate, nominating James Garfield of Ohio instead of Grant.

Grant still had money troubles. The United States provided no pension for ex-presidents, and he had barely enough money to live on. Friends and supporters in New York came to his rescue. They bought the Grants a comfortable house and provided a small trust fund.

The Grants' son, young Ulysses, was in a partnership with Ferdinand Ward, a man who was considered an investment genius. The Grants invested their money in Grant and Ward, and they encouraged other family members and old friends to invest as well. The firm paid some dividends, but one day Ferdinand

Grant (at center with white top hat) is surrounded by his family, including four of his grandchildren.

Ward disappeared, and so did all the money. He had never invested the money, but had spent it on himself. Ward was later tried and convicted and sentenced to ten years in jail for his crime.

Once again, Grant was ruined financially. He was forced to sell many of his possessions, including memorabilia from his service in the Civil War. He also had to accept help from some old friends. What hurt most were some peoples' suspicions that he had known about Ward's activities.

Grant the Writer

In 1881, Grant was asked to write an article about the battle of Shiloh for the *Century* magazine. It was so successful that he soon published articles on other

A Special Friendship

Samuel Clemens first saw Grant at an army reunion in Chicago. One night in a theater, soldiers began cheering Grant and demanding a speech. Finally, after long minutes of cheering, Grant stood up, saluted the crowd, and sat down again. Clemens was impressed by Grant's self-control and modesty. The two men met and discovered they had similar views on many issues. They also shared a sense of humor and had no patience with people who were impressed with their own importance. They remained close friends until Grant's death.

☆ ☆ ☆

Samuel Clemens (who wrote under the name Mark Twain) became Grant's friend and publisher. After Grant's death, Clemens published Grant's memoirs in two large volumes. The work was so popular that it supported Grant's family for many years.

incidents during the war. The magazine's publishers suggested he write his memoirs. Grant was about to agree when he had a visit from Samuel Clemens, the famous author who wrote under the name Mark Twain. His books *Tom Sawyer* and *Huckleberry Finn* had made him both famous and rich. Clemens was amazed at how little the publishers were offering Grant. He offered to publish Grant's memoirs himself and to pay much more generously. In February of 1885, they signed a contract.

The Final Battle

As Grant set to work on his memoirs, his family noticed that he looked ill. His throat was sore, and he sometimes had trouble swallowing. Late in the summer, he saw a doctor. It was throat cancer, probably caused by the cigars Grant had smoked for years. There was no treatment that could reverse the disease.

Writing his memoirs became a race against time. Grant desperately wanted to finish them so that Julia and their family would have some financial security after he died. With the same determination that won battles during the war, he went to work. He verified dates and checked facts, not satisfied unless everything was perfect. Sometimes he refused painkillers so that he could keep his mind clear. On a good day he might write 25 to 50 pages.

In June 1885, the family moved to a house in Mount McGregor, New York. They hoped that the mountain air might help Grant. Now breathing was becoming very difficult and he could barely walk. He worked propped up on two chairs, with a scarf around his throat to ease the pain. Eventually he couldn't talk at all and had to write notes to everyone. On July 18, the last of the manuscript was delivered to his publisher. On July 23, he died.

The book was both a popular and a literary success. Critics praised the straightforward, clear writing style. A year after its publication, Clemens presented Julia with a check for $200,000. Eventually *The Personal Memoirs of U.S. Grant* would sell more than 300,000 copies and earn nearly $450,000 for Grant's family.

Grant's funeral was held in New York City. The funeral procession was the largest ever seen in New York and took five hours to pass. Crowds of spectators

Gravely ill with throat cancer, Grant sits on the veranda of a mountain cottage, finishing the last pages of his memoirs.

watched almost silently. Two Union generals, William T. Sherman and Philip Sheridan, and two Confederate generals, Simon Buckner and Joseph E. Johnston, were the pallbearers. Eventually a huge marble and granite tomb was built for Grant in a park overlooking the Hudson River in New York City.

Chapter 6

General and President

Grant's place in history is secure as one of the greatest generals of his era. His strategies and battle tactics are still studied in military schools. His place in history as a president is less secure. Many have considered his presidency a failure. Yet a close look reveals some genuine, lasting accomplishments.

Justice for All

The task of reuniting the North and the South following the Civil War was one of the most difficult ever faced by any president. Grant hoped to bring the two sections together while ensuring that African Americans were given full rights of citizenship. His problem, as one historian put it, was that he was "a reasonable man in an unreasonable time." Grant supported strong laws guaranteeing the rights of African

After Grant's death, an imposing tomb was built to honor him in New York City on a hill overlooking the Hudson River. It was dedicated in 1897 and still attracts thousands of visitors each year.

Americans. When white southerners refused to obey the laws, he was willing to use the power of the federal government to enforce them. In the end, however, the people and Congress tired of the long struggle, and Grant was forced to retreat, giving up the long battle to assure equal rights. African Americans did not receive many of the rights assured by the laws Grant helped pass until the 1950s and 1960s.

Grant's commitment to American Indians faltered in a similar manner. His peace program failed in the face of public anger after the Modoc killings and the massacre of General Custer and his troops. Yet his straight talk about the injustices suffered by American Indian peoples called their suffering to the attention of many Americans for the first time.

It sometimes appears that as president, Grant was an honest man surrounded by crooked friends. He remained loyal to those who had helped and supported him long after it was clear they had betrayed his administration. To those friends, this seemed a strength. To historians, it seems a serious weakness.

Building Toward the Future

In lesser-known actions, Grant did begin work on several efforts that have continued to the present day. In 1872, he established Yellowstone as the first national park. In the years to follow, the government would set aside other national parks

President Ulysses S. Grant.

and preserves to protect natural resources and to make places of natural beauty available to all.

Grant also made the first proposal for a merit system in hiring government employees. Congress granted money for a commission to study civil service reform, but it never passed the recommended laws to put the system into place. Grant did live to see the first parts of a civil service system established during the presidency of Chester A. Arthur.

An early view of the Valley of the Geysers at Yellowstone, which Grant made part of the first U.S. national park.

A Rags-to-Riches Story

During his lifetime, much of the world thought Grant perfectly symbolized the American character and the American dream. He was modest and unassuming and had suffered many hardships, yet he became a great success and gained the admiration of millions. No matter how successful he became, he remained a plain, ordinary, modest man.

Grant himself had a sense of humor about his life and all its unlikely twists and turns. A few days before his death, he wrote,

> It seems that man's destiny in this world is quite as much a mystery as it is likely to be in the next. I never thought of acquiring rank in the profession I was educated for; yet [I gained] two grades higher prefixed to the rank of General officer. . . . I certainly never had either ambition or taste for political life; yet I was twice President of the United States. If anyone had suggested the idea of my becoming an author, as they frequently did, I was not sure whether they were making sport of me or not. I have now written a book which is in the hands of the manufacturers. I ask you to keep these notes very private lest I become an authority on the treatment of diseases. I have already too many trades to be proficient at any.

The Grant Memorial in Washington, D.C., portrays Grant as a general on horseback.

After his death, some people tried to portray Grant as the greatest man of the century, pure and noble. Others dismissed him as a drunk, corrupt, incompetent who got lucky. Those who knew him ignored both assessments. On the day of his funeral, General William Sherman dismissed those who spoke ill of Grant. He said to Samuel Clemens, "Grant was no namby-pamby fool. He was a man all over, rounded and complete."

Fast Facts Ulysses S. Grant

Birth:	April 27, 1822
Birthplace:	Point Pleasant, Ohio
Parents:	Jesse and Hannah Simpson Grant
Brothers & Sisters:	Samuel Simpson (1825–1861); Clara Rachel (1828–1865); Virginia Paine (1832–?); Orvil Lynch (1835–1881); Mary Frances (1839–?)
Education:	United States Military Academy, West Point, NY, graduated 1843
Occupation:	Military officer, farmer
Marriage:	To Julia Dent, August 22, 1848
Children:	(see First Lady Fast Facts, next page)
Political Party:	Republican
Public Offices:	1869–1877 18th President of the United States
His Vice Presidents:	Schuyler Colfax (1869–1873); Henry Wilson (1873–1875)
Major Actions as President:	1869 Ordered sale of government gold on "Black Friday," ending investor scheme to corner market, but ruining many investors
	1870 15th Amendment ratified, granting voting rights to African Americans
	1871 Signed Ku Klux Klan Act, providing federal enforcement against Klan and other terrorist groups
	1871 Signed Treaty of Washington, settling war claims against Great Britain
	1874 Sent federal troops to New Orleans to defeat uprising by the White League against Republican government
	1875 Signed Civil Rights Act of 1875, assuring civil rights to African Americans (declared unconstitutional 1883)
	1876 Ordered U.S. Army to pursue Sioux after massacre of General Custer and his troops
Death:	July 23, 1885
Age at Death:	63 years
Burial Place:	Grant's Tomb, Riverside Park, New York, NY

96

Fast Facts   Julia Dent Grant

Birth:	January 26, 1826
Birthplace:	White Haven plantation, Missouri
Parents:	Frederick and Ellen Bray Wrenshall Dent
Brothers & Sisters:	Four brothers and three sisters
Education:	Mauro Boarding School
Marriage:	To Ulysses S. Grant, August 22, 1848
Children:	Frederick Dent (1850–1912)
	Ulysses S. Jr. (1852–1929)
	Ellen Wrenshall (1855–1922)
	Jesse Root (1858–1934)
Death:	December 14, 1902
Age at Death:	76 years
Burial Place:	Grant's Tomb, Riverside Park, New York, NY

Timeline

1822	1839	1843	1844	1846
Hiram Ulysses Grant is born in Point Pleasant, Ohio; family moves to Georgetown, Ohio, the next year.	Grant enrolls in U.S. Military Academy, which changes his name to Ulysses S. Grant.	Graduates from West Point; stationed at Jefferson Barracks, near St. Louis.	Meets Julia Dent; is transferred to Louisiana.	Fights in U.S.-Mexican War, wins commendation at Battle of Monterrey.

1860	1861	1862	1863	1864
Family moves to Galena, Illinois, where Grant works in his father's store.	Civil War begins; Grant helps recruit volunteers in Galena; sees first action at Belmont, Missouri; promoted to brigadier general.	Commands troops that capture Fort Donelson, TN, February; commands in victory at Shiloh, TN, April.	After long campaign, captures Confederate army at Vicksburg, MS, July; relieves the siege of a Union army at Chattanooga, November.	Appointed general in chief of the Union Army; directs Overland Campaign in northern Virginia, May–June.

1871	1872	1873	1875	1877
Signs the Ku Klux Klan Act, providing federal enforcement against terrorist group, April; Treaty of Washington ratified, June.	Establishes Yellowstone as the first U.S. national park, March; elected to second term, November.	A severe panic, or recession, begins, September.	Signs Civil Rights Act, ensuring civil rights for African Americans (later ruled unconstitutional).	Leaves office; begins an extensive world tour with Julia and youngest son.

1848	1852	1854	1856	1858
Marries Julia Dent; stationed in Michigan and New York State.	Grant ordered to Fort Vancouver in Pacific Northwest, leaving Julia in the Midwest.	Resigns from the army.	Family moves to Hardscrabble in Missouri, where Grant tries farming.	Family moves into White Haven, Julia's childhood home.

1865	1867	1868	1869	1870
Grant captures Confederate capital at Richmond, April 3; Lee's army surrenders, April 9; President Lincoln is shot, dies April 15.	Serves temporarily as secretary of war under President Andrew Johnson.	Gains Republican nomination for president, is elected.	Inaugurated, March; takes action to end gold scheme, September.	Fifteenth Amendment ratified, guaranteeing African Americans the right to vote.

1879	1880	1881	1884	1885
The Grants return to the United States.	Grant contends for Republican presidential nomination, but is defeated.	Faces financial ruin when his son's investment firm fails.	Begins writing his memoirs, June; learns he has throat cancer, November.	Completes memoirs; dies July 23; huge memorial procession in New York, August; first volume of memoirs published, December.

Glossary

annex: to add a new region or territory to a country

besiege: to surround an enemy base, keeping supplies and reinforcements from reaching it

cavalry: a military unit that fights on horseback

conciliation: a process in which a dispute is settled by compromise, each side giving up some of its demands

court-martial: trial by a military court

demerit: a mark on a school record recording that a person has broken a rule or regulation

impeach: in U.S. government, to bring charges against a high official; if convicted of the charges, the official is removed from office

infantry: a military unit that fights on foot

quartermaster: a military officer responsible for providing food, clothing, and other necessities for a military unit

ratify: to approve a new law or regulation officially; constitutional amendments must be ratified by three-fourths of the states before taking effect

secede: to officially withdraw from a political unit; southern states seceded from the United States in 1860 and 1861

tanner: a workman who processes animal hides into leather

unpretentious: modest, not concerned with one's own importance

veto: in U.S. government, the refusal of a president to sign a bill passed by Congress into law; the Congress may **override** a veto by passing the bill by two-thirds majorities in both houses

Further Reading

Archer, Jules. *A House Divided: The Lives of Ulysses S. Grant and Robert E. Lee*. New York: Scholastic, 1995.

Bedwell, Randall, ed. *May I Quote You, General Grant?: Observations and Utterances of the North's Great Generals*. Nashville: Cumberland House, 1998.

Gaines, Ann Graham. *Ulysses S. Grant: Our Eighteenth President*. Chanhassen, MN: Child's World, 2002.

O'Shei, Tim. *Ulysses S. Grant: Military Leader and President*. Philadelphia: Chelsea House, 2001.

Reinert, Eric A. *Grant's Tomb*. Washington, DC: Eastern National, 1997.

Roberts, Russell. *Presidents and Scandals*. San Diego: Lucent Books, 2001.

MORE ADVANCED READING

Grant, Julia Dent. *The Personal Memoirs of Julia Dent Grant* (reprint). Carbondale, IL: Southern Illinois University Press, 1999.

Grant, Ulysses S. *Memoirs and Selected Letters*. New York: Library of America, 1990.

McConnell, Thomas. *Conversations with General Grant: An Informal Biography*. Annandale, VA: Walnut Hill Publishing Co., 1990.

Smith, Jean Edward. *Grant*. New York: Simon & Schuster, 2001.

Places to Visit

★ ★ ★ ★ ★

Grant's Birthplace State Memorial

Off U.S. Highway 52 in Point Pleasant, Ohio

P.O. Box 2

New Richmond, OH 45157

(513) 553-4911

The small house has been reconstructed and is open to visitors.

Grant's Farm

10501 Gravois Road

St. Louis, MO 63123

(314) 843-1700

Hardscrabble, the house Grant built for his family, is an exhibit at this commercial historical and wildlife preserve.

Ulysses S. Grant National Historic Site

7400 Grant Road

St. Louis, MO 63123

(314) 842-3298

The site is part of White Haven, Julia Grant's childhood home. The Grants lived at White Haven during the 1850s.

U. S. Grant Home State Historic Site

500 Bouthillier Street

Galena, IL 61036

(815) 777-3310

Attractions include the home given to Grant by the townspeople in 1865.

Grant Memorial

Washington, DC

This powerful statue of General Grant on horseback stands at the foot of Capitol Hill, between the Capitol and the National Mall.

Grant's Tomb (General Grant National Memorial)

West 122nd Street and Riverside Drive

New York, NY 10003

(212) 666-1640

This great tomb was dedicated in 1897. Located in New York City's Riverside Park, the tomb is the final resting place of Grant and his wife Julia.

Civil War Battle Sites

The National Park Service maintains many sites where Grant fought during the Civil War. Among them are:

Fort Donelson National Battlefield

Shiloh National Military Park

Vicksburg National Military Park

Fredericksburg and Spotsylvania National Military Park

Appomattox Court House

Check NPS Web sites for more information.

Online Sites of Interest

★ **Internet Public Library: Presidents of the United States (IPL-POTUS)**

www.ipl.org/div/potus/usgrant.html

A useful site providing an outline of Grant's presidency and links to other useful sites. Prepared by the School of Information at the University of Michigan.

★ **AmericanPresident.org**

http://www.americanpresident.org/history/ulyssessgrant/

A lively thumbnail biography of Grant which includes information on his military career, presidency, and family life. The site is managed by the Miller Center of Public Affairs at the University of Virginia.

★ **Grant National Historical Site**

http://www.nps.gov/ulsg

Provides background on the life of Grant and his family in Missouri during the 1850s. The site includes part of the White Haven plantation originally owned by Julia Grant's family.

★ **American Experience: Ulysses S. Grant**

http://www.pbs.org/wgbh/amex/grant/index.html

Prepared by the Public Broadcasting Service (PBS), this site provides a wealth of information about Grant and his times. The timeline is especially useful.

★ **Ulysses S. Grant Home Page**

http://www.mscomm.com/~ulysses/

An interesting collection of materials about Grant assembled by an admirer and collector. Includes many photographic portraits of Grant and details about his hobbies, interests, and family life.

Table of Presidents

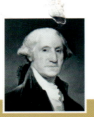 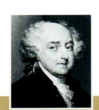  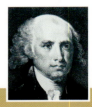

	1. George Washington	2. John Adams	3. Thomas Jefferson	4. James Madison
Took office	Apr 30 1789	Mar 4 1797	Mar 4 1801	Mar 4 1809
Left office	Mar 3 1797	Mar 3 1801	Mar 3 1809	Mar 3 1817
Birthplace	Westmoreland Co, VA	Braintree, MA	Shadwell, VA	Port Conway, VA
Birth date	Feb 22 1732	Oct 20 1735	Apr 13 1743	Mar 16 1751
Death date	Dec 14 1799	July 4 1826	July 4 1826	June 28 1836

	9. William H. Harrison	10. John Tyler	11. James K. Polk	12. Zachary Taylor
Took office	Mar 4 1841	Apr 6 1841	Mar 4 1845	Mar 5 1849
Left office	**Apr 4 1841•**	Mar 3 1845	Mar 3 1849	**July 9 1850•**
Birthplace	Berkeley, VA	Greenway, VA	Mecklenburg Co, NC	Barboursville, VA
Birth date	Feb 9 1773	Mar 29 1790	Nov 2 1795	Nov 24 1784
Death date	Apr 4 1841	Jan 18 1862	June 15 1849	July 9 1850

	17. Andrew Johnson	18. Ulysses S. Grant	19. Rutherford B. Hayes	20. James A. Garfield
Took office	Apr 15 1865	Mar 4 1869	Mar 5 1877	Mar 4 1881
Left office	Mar 3 1869	Mar 3 1877	Mar 3 1881	**Sept 19 1881•**
Birthplace	Raleigh, NC	Point Pleasant, OH	Delaware, OH	Orange, OH
Birth date	Dec 29 1808	Apr 27 1822	Oct 4 1822	Nov 19 1831
Death date	July 31 1875	July 23 1885	Jan 17 1893	Sept 19 1881

5. James Monroe	6. John Quincy Adams	7. Andrew Jackson	8. Martin Van Buren
Mar 4 1817	Mar 4 1825	Mar 4 1829	Mar 4 1837
Mar 3 1825	Mar 3 1829	Mar 3 1837	Mar 3 1841
Westmoreland Co, VA	Braintree, MA	The Waxhaws, SC	Kinderhook, NY
Apr 28 1758	July 11 1767	Mar 15 1767	Dec 5 1782
July 4 1831	Feb 23 1848	June 8 1845	July 24 1862

13. Millard Fillmore	14. Franklin Pierce	15. James Buchanan	16. Abraham Lincoln
July 9 1850	Mar 4 1853	Mar 4 1857	Mar 4 1861
Mar 3 1853	Mar 3 1857	Mar 3 1861	**Apr 15 1865•**
Locke Township, NY	Hillsborough, NH	Cove Gap, PA	Hardin Co, KY
Jan 7 1800	Nov 23 1804	Apr 23 1791	Feb 12 1809
Mar 8 1874	Oct 8 1869	June 1 1868	Apr 15 1865

21. Chester A. Arthur	22. Grover Cleveland	23. Benjamin Harrison	24. Grover Cleveland
Sept 19 1881	Mar 4 1885	Mar 4 1889	Mar 4 1893
Mar 3 1885	Mar 3 1889	Mar 3 1893	Mar 3 1897
Fairfield, VT	Caldwell, NJ	North Bend, OH	Caldwell, NJ
Oct 5 1829	Mar 18 1837	Aug 20 1833	Mar 18 1837
Nov 18 1886	June 24 1908	Mar 13 1901	June 24 1908

	25. William McKinley	**26. Theodore Roosevelt**	**27. William H. Taft**	**28. Woodrow Wilson**
Took office	Mar 4 1897	Sept 14 1901	Mar 4 1909	Mar 4 1913
Left office	**Sept 14 1901•**	Mar 3 1909	Mar 3 1913	Mar 3 1921
Birthplace	Niles, OH	New York, NY	Cincinnati, OH	Staunton, VA
Birth date	Jan 29 1843	Oct 27 1858	Sept 15 1857	Dec 28 1856
Death date	Sept 14 1901	Jan 6 1919	Mar 8 1930	Feb 3 1924

	33. Harry S. Truman	**34. Dwight D. Eisenhower**	**35. John F. Kennedy**	**36. Lyndon B. Johnson**
Took office	Apr 12 1945	Jan 20 1953	Jan 20 1961	Nov 22 1963
Left office	Jan 20 1953	Jan 20 1961	**Nov 22 1963•**	Jan 20 1969
Birthplace	Lamar, MO	Denison, TX	Brookline, MA	Johnson City, TX
Birth date	May 8 1884	Oct 14 1890	May 29 1917	Aug 27 1908
Death date	Dec 26 1972	Mar 28 1969	Nov 22 1963	Jan 22 1973

	41. George Bush	**42. Bill Clinton**	**43. George W. Bush**	
Took office	Jan 20 1989	Jan 20 1993	Jan 20 2001	
Left office	Jan 20 1993	Jan 20 2001	—	
Birthplace	Milton, MA	Hope, AR	New Haven, CT	
Birth date	June 12 1924	Aug 19 1946	July 6 1946	
Death date	—	—	—	

29. Warren G. Harding	30. Calvin Coolidge	31. Herbert Hoover	32. Franklin D. Roosevelt
Mar 4 1921	Aug 2 1923	Mar 4 1929	Mar 4 1933
Aug 2 1923•	Mar 3 1929	Mar 3 1933	**Apr 12 1945•**
Blooming Grove, OH	Plymouth, VT	West Branch, IA	Hyde Park, NY
Nov 21 1865	July 4 1872	Aug 10 1874	Jan 30 1882
Aug 2 1923	Jan 5 1933	Oct 20 1964	Apr 12 1945

37. Richard M. Nixon	38. Gerald R. Ford	39. Jimmy Carter	40. Ronald Reagan
Jan 20 1969	Aug 9 1974	Jan 20 1977	Jan 20 1981
Aug 9 1974★	Jan 20 1977	Jan 20 1981	Jan 20 1989
Yorba Linda, CA	Omaha, NE	Plains, GA	Tampico, IL
Jan 9 1913	July 14 1913	Oct 1 1924	Feb 11 1911
Apr 22 1994	—	—	—

• Indicates the president died while in office.

★ Richard Nixon resigned before his term expired.

Index

About the Author

Janet Riehecky is a full-time, freelance writer for children. Since 1988, she has published more than 90 books for children. Her books include both fiction and nonfiction and range from preschool picture books to junior high history. Her special love, though, is the intermediate reader, for whom she writes both nonfiction titles and a series of mystery novels. A resident of Illinois, she was especially pleased to write about fellow Illinois resident Ulysses S. Grant, and took the opportunity to visit his home and former workplace in Galena, Illinois; his home Hardscrabble on Grant's Farm in St. Louis, Missouri; and the Ulysses S. Grant National Historic Site in St. Louis. She wishes to thank all the tour guides who took the time to talk with her, especially the members of the Civil War Reenactors, 8th Regular Missouri Volunteers.

Ms. Riehecky did her undergraduate work at Illinois Wesleyan University and completed a master's degree in communication at Illinois State University and a master's degree in English literature at Northwestern University. Her twenty-four volume series on dinosaurs won the 1988 Summit Award for Best Children's Nonfiction. She is a popular speaker in elementary schools where she gives a variety of talks including "The Magic of Writing," which links magic tricks and illusions with tips on creative writing, and "Learning about Dinosaurs," in which she uses her extensive collection of fossils and casts of dinosaur bones to teach how scientists use these "clues" to learn about dinosaurs. Ms. Riehecky is also the national director of Kids Love a Mystery, a national literacy outreach of Mystery Writers of America.